GREAT ENTREPRENEURS IN U.S. HISTORY

Cornelius Vanderbilt

and the Railroad Industry

Therese Shea

PowerKiDS press.

New York

Published in 2017 by The Rosen Publishing Group, Inc.
29 East 21st Street, New York, NY 10010

First Edition

Editor: Sarah Machajewski
Book Design: Mickey Harmon

Photo Credits: Cover, pp. 1–6, 8–14, 16–24, 26–28, 30–32 (series design) Melodist/Shutterstock.com; cover, pp. 1, 11 (Vanderbilt) https://en.wikipedia.org/wiki/File:Cornelius_Vanderbilt_Daguerrotype2.jpg; p. 5 https://commons.wikimedia.org/wiki/File:Cornelius_Vanderbilt_three-quarter_view.jpg; p. 7 Imagno/Contributor/Hulton Archive/Getty Images; p. 7 (inset) https://en.wikipedia.org/wiki/Periauger; pp. 8–9 Everett Historical/Shutterstock.com; p. 13 SoleilC/Shutterstock.com; p. 15 https://commons.wikimedia.org/w/index.php?title=File:The_Photographic_History_of_The_Civil_War_Volume_06_Page_315.jpg&oldid=105272986; pp. 16, 27 Hulton Archive/Stringer/Hulton Archive/Getty Images; p. 17 courtesy of the Library of Congress; p. 19 UniversalImagesGroup/Contributor/Universal Images Group/Getty Images; p. 21 https://commons.wikimedia.org/wiki/File:1866_Albany_railroad_bridge.jpg; p. 23 https://upload.wikimedia.org/wikipedia/commons/thumb/2/21/Vanderbilt_%26_Fisk.jpg/1280px-Vanderbilt_%26_Fisk.jpg; p. 25 Museum of the City of New York/Contributor/Getty Images; p. 29 Sean Pavone/Shutterstock.com.

Cataloging-in-Publication Data

Names: Shea, Therese M.
Title: Cornelius Vanderbilt and the railroad industry / Therese M. Shea.
Description: New York : PowerKids Press, 2017. | Series: Great entrepreneurs in U.S. history | Includes index.
Identifiers: ISBN 9781499421194 (pbk.) | ISBN 9781499421217 (library bound) | ISBN 9781499421200 (6 pack)
Subjects: LCSH: Vanderbilt, Cornelius, 1794-1877. | Businessmen–United States–Biography–Juvenile literature. | Railroads–United States–History–Juvenile literature.
Classification: LCC CT275.V23 S44 2017 | DDC 385'.092–d23

Manufactured in the United States of America

CPSIA Compliance Information: Batch #BS16PK: For Further Information contact Rosen Publishing, New York, New York at 1-800-237-9932

Contents

Self-Made Success

Cornelius Vanderbilt isn't an easy man to describe. In his lifetime, he was admired, hated, and feared. He was called both a brilliant businessman and a pitiless robber baron. He demanded perfection of his employees, but also of himself. What is undeniable is that Vanderbilt was the first **tycoon** in the history of the United States.

Born into poverty a decade after the American Revolution (1775–1783), Vanderbilt became very wealthy by seizing the opportunities provided by the Industrial Revolution. The development of steam engines meant vehicles could transport people and goods faster than ever before. Vanderbilt founded his companies on efficiency and inexpensive transportation. Whether all his business practices were fair is a matter of **debate**, but his success isn't.

What Is a Robber Baron?

Robber barons were businessmen who held great wealth and power and sometimes acted in unfair and dishonest ways to get what they wanted. Vanderbilt was first compared to robber barons in a *New York Times* article in 1859. The writer criticized Vanderbilt for using his success to run other companies out of business. In this book, you'll learn about some of Vanderbilt's business methods. Then you can decide for yourself whether or not he was a robber baron.

The Industrial Revolution was a period of major change in the U.S. economy that also introduced power-driven machinery. Vanderbilt's businesses used this new technology.

The Young Commodore

Cornelius Vanderbilt was born on May 27, 1794, in the Port Richmond area of Staten Island, New York. His family was far from wealthy. His parents were farmers, and Cornelius was one of nine children. His father—who didn't know how to read or write—made extra money by transporting goods between Staten Island and Manhattan by boat. By the age of 11, Cornelius was helping him, spending more time on the water than at school. Cornelius was intelligent, though, and eagerly took an interest in the business side of shipping.

According to legend, by the time he was 16, Cornelius had come up with enough money to buy a two-masted sailboat called a periauger, much like his father's. He began his own business transporting people and goods around the New York City area and became a skilled sailor.

Cornelius Vanderbilt earned the nickname "Commodore" for the time he spent on New York waters. A commodore is a captain in charge of a **fleet** of ships. The nickname would stick with him his whole life.

Manhattan, early 1800s

7

Cornelius Vanderbilt's **ferry** business was a success. He charged customers a bit less than his competition. He bought more boats to add to his company. During the War of 1812, Vanderbilt received a contract from the U.S. government to bring supplies to troops stationed along the Hudson River. The year after the war began, Vanderbilt, now 19 years old, married Sophia Johnson. They had 13 children.

Steamboat travel was becoming popular around

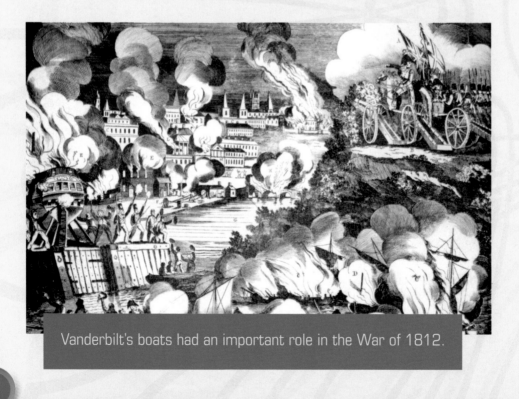

Vanderbilt's boats had an important role in the War of 1812.

this time. Steamboats used steam to power engines that moved paddle wheels or **propellers**. They were much more reliable than sailboats. Around 1817, Vanderbilt sold his boats and began working for Thomas Gibbons as a steamboat captain, ferrying people between New York and New Jersey.

His First Million

Cornelius Vanderbilt later said his time with Thomas Gibbons helped him recognize that he'd rather own a business than work for someone else. He was a captain for Gibbons until 1829. By that time, he had learned enough about the business and saved enough money to buy steamboats for his own ferry operation.

Again, Vanderbilt undercut, or charged less, than his competitors. He named his service the "People's Line." He gained a reputation as a tough businessman. By the mid-1840s, most boat traffic on the Hudson River belonged to Vanderbilt's fleet. By 1846, he was a millionaire.

Vanderbilt was so successful that other shipping companies paid him to stop working on the Hudson River! He then began transporting passengers and goods between Long Island, New York; Boston, Massachusetts; and Providence, Rhode Island.

Gibbons v. Ogden

In the 1820s, Thomas Gibbons fought a **monopoly** on the New York waterways. New York State had given a group of businessmen total control over steamboat travel to New Jersey. Gibbons wanted to do business between New York and New Jersey, so he took his case to the U.S. Supreme Court. The case *Gibbons v. Ogden* was decided in Gibbons's favor in 1824. The court said state governments couldn't make decisions about business that happened across state lines, and the monopoly was broken.

This is the earliest known daguerreotype of Cornelius Vanderbilt, from around 1845. A daguerreotype is an early form of photograph.

The California Gold Rush

In the late 1840s, Cornelius Vanderbilt formed another transportation company. His Accessory Transit Company took people from New York City to San Francisco, California. The route took passengers through Nicaragua in Central America.

With the discovery of gold in California in 1848, a rush of people hoping to strike it rich sought to head west as quickly as possible. Vanderbilt's service was one of the fastest ways to get there—and the most inexpensive. While other companies charged $600 a trip, passage on Accessory Transit cost about $400. Vanderbilt's company was immediately successful, making about $26 million annually in today's money.

Once again, Vanderbilt dominated the industry to such an extent that his competitors paid him to stop! They gave him a monthly sum of $40,000—later $56,000—to halt his operation.

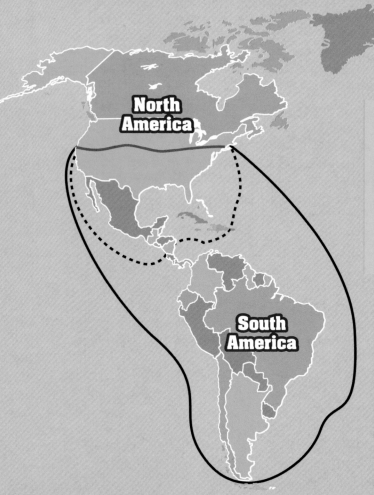

North America

South America

Cape Horn route (6 to 8 months)	——————
Nicaragua route (about 1 month)	··········
overland route (4 to 6 months)	——————

At the time of the California gold rush, there were no cars and no cross-country trains. Vanderbilt's route through Nicaragua, which is north of Panama, was a shorter distance than other routes.

A Tough Way to Travel

The Accessory Transit Company wasn't a luxurious way to travel. One passenger wrote to Vanderbilt in a letter published in the *New York Times*: "The meats set before us at our meals were...unfit as food....Our eyes never feasted by the appearance of a clean cloth on the table, nor...upon a clean sheet or pillow case. Not a bathroom on the ship....We will teach our children to revere your name as the most successful, most **penurious**, and most heartless millionaire that ever disgraced our country."

The Civil War

One of Vanderbilt's steamboats—the *Vanderbilt*—played a part in the American Civil War. A Confederate ironclad, which is a wooden warship covered in metal, was attacking Union vessels. Cannonballs had no effect on the *Virginia*. The Union's ironclad, the *Monitor*, was the only ship that could battle with it, and their clash, called the Battle of Hampton Roads, ended in a draw. The Union forces were in trouble if the *Virginia* broke out of the **blockade** that was in place.

In 1862, U.S. President Abraham Lincoln and Secretary of War Edwin Stanton asked Vanderbilt to rent the *Vanderbilt* to them. Instead of asking for payment, Vanderbilt donated the ship, his largest and fastest, to the Union navy. In preparation for war, its bow was fitted with a steel ram.

The *Vanderbilt* was 355 feet (108 m) long, with giant paddle wheels and two smokestacks.

The Patriot

Vanderbilt had tried to give his ship to the Union when the war started. He insisted on turning it into a warship himself. The *Times* newspaper of London reported: "Her steam machinery has been protected by rails...her prow has been armed with a...nose, with the intention to poke right into the side of the [*Virginia*]....Its edge is made of steel, and very sharp." The *Virginia* was later destroyed by its own crew so it wouldn't be captured by the Union.

15

Building a Railroad Empire

In the mid-1800s, railroads were quickly becoming a major transportation system. More tracks were being built, and passengers and goods were traveling faster than ever before. However, at that time, this type of travel consisted of mostly small railroads with local lines. To travel farther than a rail line, passengers and goods had to get off one train line and hop on another that could take them farther.

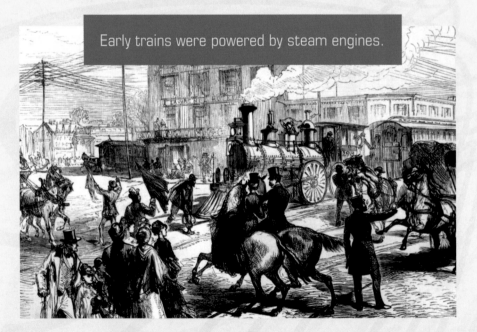

Early trains were powered by steam engines.

The trains ran at all different times. It was a difficult, confusing way to travel.

Cornelius Vanderbilt saw an opportunity. He began buying **stock** in small railroad companies in New York until he owned enough to control them. By consolidating, or joining, his various railroads, Vanderbilt made traveling by train much more efficient and inexpensive. It was the start of his railroad empire.

In 1863, Vanderbilt took control of the New York and Harlem Railroad, which ran from Manhattan to Harlem and to Chatham, New York. Under the management of his son William, the once-suffering line was praised for its cleanliness and timeliness.

Next, Cornelius Vanderbilt began buying stock in the Hudson River Railroad and the New York Central Railroad. He also provided the money for the construction of a railroad bridge over the Hudson River near Albany, New York. Before that bridge was built, passengers on the Hudson River Railroad had to get off the train and cross the river by steamboat in summer or horse-drawn sled in winter to connect with the New York Central. Those vehicles would no longer be needed.

A Head for Business

Vanderbilt's oldest son, William or "Billy," assisted his father with the railroad business. Early in his life, William had been a disappointment to his father, who saw him as weak and unmotivated. After William turned a failing farm into a successful venture, though, his father took notice. Vanderbilt gave his son control over the Long Island Rail Road Company, and he turned that into a success, too. William went on to double his father's fortune, though he lived only eight years after his father's death.

William Vanderbilt is shown here in a political cartoon. His size, towering over the other railroad businessmen, is meant to show his great power.

Playing Tough

Some New York Central Railroad investors began buying shares of the company to take control from Vanderbilt. They backed out of agreements with him, too. So, Vanderbilt closed his bridge, refusing to allow the trains to cross. Passengers were forced to walk across the frozen river, while freight just piled up. The railroad began losing money so fast that Vanderbilt's enemies gave up their shares. Vanderbilt bought enough shares—at a cheap price—to take control of New York Central. In 1869, he consolidated the New York Central and Hudson River Railroads.

When the New York State Senate's Railroad Committee questioned him about shutting down the Albany bridge, Vanderbilt said: "I have always served the public to the best of my ability...it is in my interest to do so....The law, as I view it, goes too slow for me when I have the remedy in my own hands."

Playing the Market

Vanderbilt was a skillful player in the stock market. He was one of the first people to carry out stock splits, which means increasing the amount of stock in a company by issuing more shares. Each share is then worth less but creates an opportunity for more shareholders and, therefore, more profits. Companies still perform stock splits today. The majority of Vanderbilt's wealth came from stocks and **bonds** in his railroads.

Vanderbilt's actions had cut off New York City from the rest of the world. The Albany bridge matter began a debate in the country about whether businesses (and businessmen) should be able to act in ways that can disrupt people's lives.

The Erie War

In the 1860s, Cornelius Vanderbilt also turned his attention to buying the Erie Railroad, which would connect his New York lines to Chicago, Illinois. At that time, the railroad was controlled by businessman Daniel Drew. At first, Drew supported Vanderbilt. However, he and two other businessmen, Jay Gould and Jim Fisk, turned against Vanderbilt. They began issuing more stock in the Erie Railroad—illegally. This move reduced the worth of Vanderbilt's shares. Still, he kept buying this "**watered stock**."

After Drew, Gould, and Fisk were ordered to settle the matter in New York State court, they escaped to New Jersey in 1868. In the end, Gould and Fisk took control of the railroad. Gould was said to have paid off New York lawmakers in order to get out of trouble. Vanderbilt never added the Erie to his railway empire.

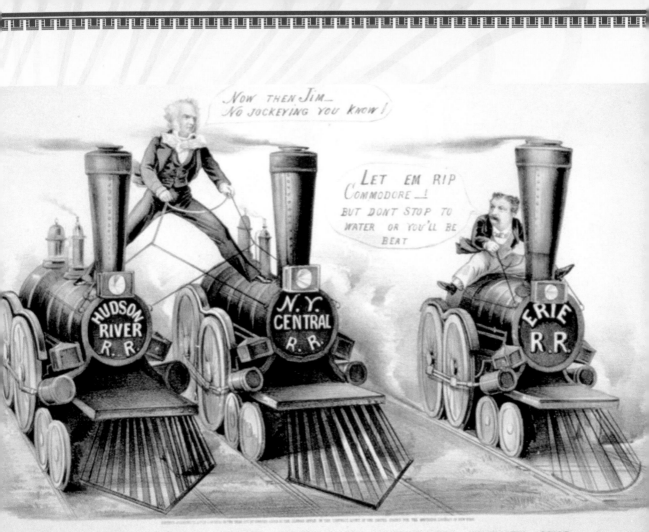

THE GREAT RACE FOR THE WESTERN STAKES 1870

The American public was fascinated by what became known as the "Erie War." Cartoons like this filled them in on the latest dealings of the millionaires.

The Empire Rolls On

As time passed, it soon became clear—the Vanderbilt rail empire was unstoppable. In the early 1870s, William Vanderbilt oversaw the acquisition of the Lake Shore and Michigan Southern Railroad, beginning the first rail service from New York City to Chicago, Illinois. The Vanderbilts had created the largest railway system in the United States.

By this time, William Vanderbilt was the one in power, though many people believed his father was still in charge. This was important, especially when the stock market was particularly unstable in 1873. Even people who disliked Cornelius Vanderbilt believed that he was a talented businessman. They were confident that his decisions would keep the money they invested in his companies safe.

Vanderbilt's Grand Central Depot is pictured here.

Grand Central Depot

In 1869, the Vanderbilts bought 23 acres (9 ha) of land outside New York City. They built a rail station called Grand Central Depot for their New York lines. Later, the growth of New York City meant the noisy, busy depot was in the middle of the city. It was remade into the beautiful Grand Central Terminal, which opened in 1913. A statue of Cornelius Vanderbilt still stands outside Grand Central Terminal today.

Entering the Oil Boom

Oil was discovered to be an excellent source of fuel in the 19th century. Soon, companies were formed to locate and collect oil. The nation's rail lines competed to transport the valuable liquid.

In 1868, John D. Rockefeller's Standard Oil Company created a deal in which Standard Oil would use Lake Shore Railroad's trains to transport oil at a reduced price. The agreement guaranteed Vanderbilt freight on his trains and allowed Rockefeller to keep the costs of his oil products lower than his competition.

Rockefeller bought up many competitors' companies until he controlled about 90 percent of the nation's oil. He later tried to get an even better deal from other railroad companies. This angered Vanderbilt, who later joined with his competitors against Rockefeller.

The U.S. government made John D. Rockefeller's Standard Oil break into many smaller companies in 1911, as it was a near monopoly.

The Man Who Shaped Industries

Cornelius Vanderbilt died at the age 82 on January 4, 1877, in Manhattan. He was buried in New Dorp, Staten Island. His estate was worth more than $100 million, which was more than the U.S. Treasury held at that time. He left most of his fortune to William in his will. The remaining amount he divided among his wife and other surviving children. Further generations of Vanderbilts became known for their luxurious mansions and extravagant spending, a contrast from how Cornelius lived his life.

Cornelius Vanderbilt began his life in poverty and made his fortune twice, through his steamboat empire and through his railroad lines. No doubt, the businesses he built shaped both the U.S. landscape and its economy for years to come.

Vanderbilt University

Cornelius's wife Sophia died in 1868. The next year, Cornelius married a distant cousin named Frank Armstrong Crawford, a woman 44 years younger than him. Under her influence, Cornelius did something he rarely did—donated money. He gave a large sum—$1 million—to Central University in Tennessee. It was the largest charitable donation in the nation's history at that time and is worth $18 million in today's money. The school changed its name to Vanderbilt University. Today, its sports teams are named the "Commodores" for him.

A Timeline of Cornelius Vanderbilt's Life

1794 — Cornelius Vanderbilt is born in Staten Island, New York.

1810 — Cornelius buys a periauger and begins a transportation business.

1817 — Vanderbilt sells his boats and begins working for Thomas Gibbons as a steamboat captain.

1829 — Vanderbilt leaves Gibbons to begin his own ferry operation.

1846 — Vanderbilt becomes a millionaire.

late 1840s — Vanderbilt's Accessory Transit Company is formed, transporting people to the California gold rush.

1862 — President Abraham Lincoln and Secretary of War Edwin Stanton ask Vanderbilt to hire out his ship the *Vanderbilt*.

1863 — Vanderbilt takes control of the New York and Harlem Railroad, beginning his railroad empire.

1868 — John D. Rockefeller, owner of Standard Oil, strikes a deal to transport oil on Vanderbilt's trains.

1869 — Vanderbilt marries Frank Armstrong Crawford.

1870s — The Vanderbilts' railroads offer the first rail service between New York City and Chicago, Illinois.

1873 — Vanderbilt donates $1 million to Central University, which is renamed after him.

1877 — Vanderbilt dies in Manhattan, New York.

Glossary

blockade: An act of war in which one side uses ships to stop people or supplies from entering or leaving an area.

bond: A document in which a government or company promises to pay back an amount of money that it has borrowed and to pay interest on the borrowed money.

debate: A talk between people whose opinions are different.

ferry: To carry or move someone or something on a boat, usually for a short distance between two places. A ferry is also a kind of boat that does this.

fleet: A group of ships or vehicles that move or work together or that are controlled or owned by one company.

monopoly: Complete ownership or control of the entire supply of goods or services in an industry.

penurious: Not generous with money.

propellers: Paddle-like parts on a ship that spin in the water to move the ship forward.

stock: A share of the value of a company which can be bought, sold, or traded as an investment.

tycoon: A person who has collected great wealth and power in business.

watered stock: Stock that is sold with a value that is much greater than its actual value.

Index

Due to the changing nature of Internet links, PowerKids Press has developed an online list of websites related to the subject of this book. This site is updated regularly. Please use this link to access the list: www.powerkidslinks.com/entre/vand